ROYAL COMMISSION ON THE PRESS

Minority Report

THE LABOUR PARTY
September 1977

ISBN 0 86117 001 6

FOREWORD

The Labour Party has decided to re-publish as a pamphlet the Minority Report of the Royal Commission on the Press.

This may be regarded as a somewhat unusual step; but we are doing so because we believe that this important minority view has not so far been given the attention it merits.

We believe the Minority Report contains an extremely important analysis of the state of Britain's press. It also includes proposals which, though they do not go as far as those put forward in the Labour Party's evidence to the Royal Commission, none the less reveal constructive thinking about the future of the press.

It is worth recalling that the Minority Report received little attention from the press when the Royal Commission report was published in July. In fact some national newspapers managed virtually to ignore its existence.

The majority report was of course warmly received by most of the newspapers — no doubt because it was so bland and complaisant.

One thing is quite certain. There is very little in the majority report to encourage a continuing dialogue on the future of Britain's press. One must turn to the Minority Report for that.

The Labour Party believes that there is a strong political bias in the press against the Labour Party and against socialist ideas. The Minority Report shares that view.

But it is not simply on those grounds that we believe the Minority Report represents the basis for a wide-ranging debate on the future shape of the press.

The report, signed by David Basnett and Geoffrey Goodman, presents a critique of the political and cultural imbalance of the press in a much wider setting. It argues for greater diversity to help inform a greater number of people about the changes now taking place in our society. It wants to see the press playing a stronger role in a developing democratic system. It sees great dangers in the current trend and the commercial pressures which are turning some of our popular newspapers into sheets of trivia and pure entertainment.

We believe these are reasons which amply justify our re-publishing the Minority Report. Let the debate continue. It can do nothing but good for those who genuinely believe in establishing a more democratic press in Britain.

Ron Hayward
General Secretary

ROYAL COMMISSION ON THE PRESS
Minority Report

1   It is necessary to emphasise at the outset that the signatories to this minority view find no satisfaction in separating themselves from the majority of the Commission. This is not a posture of dissent taken eagerly or from any assumption that there is particular virtue in minority opinion. It would have been altogether preferable for the Commission to have been able to offer a unanimous report. Unfortunately that has not been possible.

2   We could not accept the majority view for one very simple reason: we do not believe it deals with sufficient strength and urgency with the dangers facing the British press. In terms both of the economic and democratic development of the press there are dangers that are apparent *now* but which in our view will become infinitely more so by the early 1980s. We believe it is the duty of this third post-war Royal Commission on the Press to cast their vision beyond the immediate crisis in the press, serious enough though that is, and consider the implications of the situation for the longer-term future of a democratic press in Britain.

3   Nor is it enough to advocate, as we do in the majority report as well as in the interim report, reforms in the financial, technological and manpower structure of the industry vital though they are. Neither is it enough merely to consider improving the industrial relations atmosphere with changes in the institutional framework of management/labour relations. These are of course areas of great importance but they ought to be seen as part of a wider problem which is: the nature and character of our press. We believe the British press is not as bad as many of its critics claim, but we also believe it is still far from good enough to cope with the variety of social, economic and cultural challenges which our society is now experiencing and which, in our view, it will face with increasing tensions during the next decade. To take but one specific and recent question— the incident concerning the *Daily Mail* story on British Leyland's 'slush-fund'. The failure of the Commission to deal adequately

4

with the attacks on Lord Ryder (in the *Daily Mail*)—to which we refer at greater length in paragraph 11—shows that the majority report, in our view, has not sufficiently taken into account the dangerous way in which the press has been, and is, developing. We believe the Commission should have responded more positively to the Prime Minister's request at that time.

4   In one chapter (Chapter 20), that on the Press Council, there are important proposals which if carried out would certainly contribute to improving the performance of the press. We agree with these proposals although in some cases we would have preferred them to have been even stronger. We also agree with much else in the report as it stands. A great deal of the analysis about the press is excellent and we would not wish to demur from any of this. Many of the existing recommendations are fully acceptable to us, although in some chapters we believe there is an imbalance and a timidity which tends to harm the perspective of the report. For example, we would have preferred to see more radical reforms proposed for the newspaper distribution industry. None the less, we do accept a large measure of what is contained in the majority view. Our complaint is that when drawn together the matrix of these proposals and recommendations, as well as the analysis, only go to emphasise the need, in our view, for further reforms. Reforms which we suggest could contribute towards improving the character of the press and encouraging the expansion in its diversity. The expansion of diversity is in our view crucial to genuine freedom of the press. We might quote a line from the Commission Working Paper No 2* in which it is emphasised that 'the more diversity, the more competition, the more likely that the best ideas will find a home in people's minds and be disseminated most widely and quickly'.

5   We recognise that in setting out some of the flaws in the press we will rightly be challenged to put forward positive proposals which might help to correct and improve the newspapers. We will try to do this although we must emphasise, at the outset, that we will disappoint many people because there are no perfect solutions, certainly no magic formulae. We have

*Review of Sociological Writing on the Press, Professor D McQuail, RCP, Working Paper No 2, page 10.

some thoughts on what we believe could be done to help improve the press. But we do this not because we hold them to be total or even novel solutions as such—but, rather as contributions, small experimental steps, towards a better press.

6   Our general stand is based on the view that market pressures now increasingly imposing themselves on the national press constitute a serious impediment to existing diversity, and an even greater one to hopes of expanding upon that diversity. It is not necessary for us to enlarge in detail on this proposition because we believe the evidence already produced in the body of the main report and the analysis contained in it illustrates the point with sufficient force. Everyone is aware of the crucial importance of advertising revenue in underpinning the commercial viability of newspapers: everyone is aware of the relationship between large circulation popular newspapers and their need to attract sufficient advertising. Everyone is also now aware of the pressures that this increasingly involves in terms of circulation war and the threat this carries to social and ethical standards. Of course the vigour of these market pressures certainly helps to foster enterprise. Yet in our view what these pressures are also doing is to diminish the stature of much that is excellent in popular journalism, and to emphasise and highlight, that which is questionable if not objectionable and even obscene. These remarks should not be read as an indiscriminate attack on all market enterprise in journalism; a free and democratic press requires such enterprise if it is to remain independent of complete reliance on the state. But it is important to reflect on the damage that can be (and is) done to the credibility of the press when such enterprise runs amok. We see serious danger that the competitive pressures now imposing themselves on the national (and provincial) press will diminish its diversity as well as its genuine independence and credibility. We think it is important to state that there is nothing inherently virtuous in a massive circulation for its own sake—provided a lesser one can be made economically viable while maintaining professional standards. This is not an easy goal but we believe it to be possible.

7   Indeed, in the analysis of the problem we find ourselves supported by the majority report which states, 'we have no doubt

that there is a gap in political terms which could be filled with advantage. However, no one knows whether the readership of such a paper would enable it to survive commercially'.

8 We are in agreement with that analysis. Where we depart from the majority is that they are not prepared to suggest measures which would at least try to overcome these commercial obstacles.

The Current Scene

9 We have in Britain a highly adult and politically mature populace whose main source of news and current affairs information now comes increasingly from TV and radio. This has been made inevitable in the last 10 to 15 years as a result of the communications revolution which has brought the TV screen into almost every home. The cultural and social impact of this, quite dramatic, change as well as the spread of local and commercial radio, has still not been fully understood. Our main concern in this Minority Report is to ensure that the written word in terms of news and information does not wither by default under the combined impact of commercial pressures and the communications revolution. We believe that newspapers are and will remain for the foreseeable future fundamental to any fully informed democracy. The immediacy of TV/radio news and current affairs reporting is of self-evident impact. But there remains the absolute need for the balanced perspectives of the written word. We do not see these as competing forces: rather as complementary ones. In a civilised society they ought to be partners in the enormous task of keeping people fully informed about the nature and problems of contemporary domestic and world affairs. We say all this at the risk of sounding pompous. So be it. But we say it because we are convinced not only of its importance to the functioning of a healthy democratic society, but because of the dangers now threatening it.

10 We are convinced that there is a serious danger that the broad mass of people could before long find themselves without a reasonably economic, as well as responsible, popular press.

The danger of polarisation, once held up by that Cassandra of the future, Mr Cecil King, is in fact much closer than he himself might have believed. The gap between the two poles is widening. At one extreme the excellence of some of our quality newspapers and at the other edge the vacuity and irresponsibility of some of our popular newspapers is now more glaring than ever. We do not suggest that these tendencies can be altogether avoided. We certainly are not advocating a stereotyped, dull, prissy press: nor are we in any sense deploring the lively, entertaining, highly professional popular daily papers. But we do believe that there is a cultural gap between the two extremes which is unhealthy for our democracy. We believe there is room for what we might call a 'third force' in the press, and we are convinced that this need, if it is to be satisfied, is unlikely to obtain sufficient encouragement from conventional market forces. Certainly if the third force is to contain a paper of the left to help correct the political and cultural imbalance which the majority report recognises, then the market alone is unlikely to provide it.

11   To launch and sustain such newspapers in the prevailing economic environment is a hazardous undertaking. It is certainly discouraging to those, like the trade unions, who would otherwise wish to experiment with a new newspaper of the left. Yet we believe it is of crucial importance that steps need to be taken to encourage a better political balance in Britain's press. We cannot accept the complacency of the majority report regarding political bias. The failure of the Commission to fully discuss the implications of the *Daily Mail's* attacks on Lord Ryder and its refusal to re-consider its recommendations and conclusions (despite an appeal by the Prime Minister) underline this belief. The decision by a leading national newspaper to publish serious accusations on the basis of a forgery can only have been made because of political motives. The attack on Lord Ryder, the National Enterprise Board and British Leyland was another attempt to discredit publicly-owned institutions. Despite the many scandals in private industry—which have been at least equally as serious as the allegations made against Lord Ryder and the NEB—few have received such coverage in the popular press as the *Daily Mail* gave to the slanders against Lord Ryder. The failure of the majority report to encourage some positive steps towards increasing press diversity must therefore be

regretted. To be content to leave the situation entirely as it is can only increase the dangers. It leaves the major area of the national press under the dominant influence of those who will be tempted to pursue politically motivated attacks in an irresponsible manner. The problem is that political bias is largely one-sided. There is no balance of political irresponsibility. Nor are we advocating such a depressing solution. We are simply putting forward a case for offering *positive* encouragement towards a broader political balance and therefore, we would hope, greater political responsibility. Our chief complaint about Chapter 10 of the main report is that the scope of the research carried out was too limited. The research was not called on to consider bias in a form that would have demonstrated what we believe to be a manifest political imbalance in Britain's national press. We are therefore surprised, to say the least, at the complacency of the majority view on this issue.

12   It could be argued that if as we claim our society is so adult and politically mature why then is it necessary to consider any form of artificial stimulation to newspaper development? This in our view is an over simplification. Commercial pressures are frequently often too powerful in exploiting a popular taste for trivia to be left completely to their own devices. The bad and the shoddy often tend to drive out the good and the quality. That is not the same thing as saying that people do not want to read good newspapers or that if people wished to do so the market would automatically respond to meet the need.

13   It is our view that in all spheres of our national life the focus of change tends to be on the increasing demand by people for more involvement and greater participation. For instance, the pressure for political devolution as well as industrial democracy; for educational reform, for race and sex equality, etc. These pressure groups which have risen to become important forces in our society do not seem to be adequately reflected in the changes (or the absence of changes) in the media. To be sure if these movements for social change are to be effectively equipped with knowledge and information that would enable them to reach balanced judgements, we believe they require a better and certainly more diverse press.

14   So we return to the crucial question: if we are justified in believing that these propositions have some validity, how can we help to encourage a greater diversity without jeopardising the independence and freedoms of a democratic press? There is no point in trying to avoid this central dilemma.

15   We fully recognise that any form of state intervention must carry enormous risks and dangers. We know that it is this spectre which has deterred the majority of Commission Members from going further with some of their proposals and recommendations, particularly in respect of diversity and encouraging new entrants into the press, though we believe most of them share our general concern. We believe that the majority feel that the risks attached to any form of government assistance or intervention are greater than leaving the situation as it is. We understand and respect that view, but we cannot wholly share it. This is because we believe that the dangers now in existence and those likely to emerge with still greater force in the future are so strong that some risks, certainly some experiments need to be taken. They are risks which, we feel, are minimal and would certainly be constantly under public and parliamentary surveillance.

16   The Majority Report states in (Chapter 13, paragraph 13.47) that it rejects 'all the proposals for government assistance which have been put to us'. Not least because of the difficulties involved in discriminating 'like a censor between one applicant and another'. The majority argue that those who propose some form of intervention underestimate the problems of avoiding such censorship. We do not accept this view. In fact we would claim that the majority have overstated these problems and consequently overestimated the dangers involved in pursuing forms of action along the lines we are advocating. Moreover we believe that our own modest proposals do in fact avoid the objectionable features of discrimination and, certainly, of censorship.

17   There is no virtue in exaggerating the perils of state intervention as if they were the only threats on the horizon. The disenfranchisement of a great mass of popular newspaper readership could be a peril of at least equal magnitude. However,

to avoid any misunderstanding, it is perhaps necessary for us to state categorically that we are totally committed to press freedom and the need not only for its preservation but its expansion. We are convinced that these freedoms remain a basic condition for a healthy democracy. What we are seeking to point out here is that there is no golden rule which can guarantee this. The market system can no more be relied on as a protector of these freedoms than can the state. Much that is valuable in journalism tends to be distorted and debased by the contemporary pressures of the market. Nor can the state be relied on to ensure the protection of these freedoms and values. At the same time government intervention ought not to be regarded automatically as leading inescapably to the suppression of democratic values and higher standards of journalism so long as there remain powerful checks against the abuse of such intervention. There is, for instance, a great deal of evidence to support the view that the kind of relationship established, however painfully, over the years between government and BBC, has led to higher standards of broadcasting and the dissemination of cultural values which would have been absent and broadcasting been left entirely to the whims of the market. Despite all the criticisms levelled at it, the BBC remains probably the best broadcasting institution in the world. We make this point simply to underline that government intervention is not automatically or necessarily an evil.

18   We would also draw attention to a recent study by Political and Economic Planning* which analysed subsidies to the press in 13 European countries. In all instances there is some form of government assistance to help sustain a diverse and democratic press. In all cases, as the PEP report states: 'there has been grave heart-searching as to whether such a subsidy might defeat its own object and create avenues of government or official interference in content. In no country, however, in which subsidies have been introduced has anyone complained that governments have interfered or tried to interfere more, afterwards, than before'.

19   In seeking a positive solution we have borne in mind the above arguments: we have concluded that there *is* a gap in the

Subsidies and the Press in Europe by Anthony Smith — Political and Economic Planning.

press, which has been created by the intense competition amongst newspapers, and which the market system now or in the future is unlikely to fill. And that there is therefore a need for a degree of state intervention to provide the resources—or at least assist in so doing—to help achieve a better balance, provided that sufficient limitations are put on that intervention to ensure that the state does not threaten the essential freedom of the press.

Possible Remedies

20 It is often suggested that the strides now being taken towards a new press technology will of itself help to stimulate a greater diversity. The reasoning behind this is that the new technology will cheapen production costs and produce a surplus of printing capacity that will encourage a wider use of these available resources. It is possible that this could happen. Certainly there is a current surplus of capacity and the signs are that this surplus will continue and may even increase. This tendency will of course become stronger if the growth of press monopoly continues. It has been suggested to us that the existence of such a surplus renders the concept of a National Printing Corporation redundant. But let us consider an equally plausible alternative course of development. This runs as follows: the cost of new technology is unlikely to lead to any significant change in the existing pattern of ownership. Moreover, the surplus capacity might conceivably be prohibited from use by competing new entrant newspapers (this danger was evident in the negotiations between Beaverbrook Newspapers and Associated Newspapers). It is therefore likely that new production methods lead to an even greater concentration of plant ownership especially if costs escalate as seems probable. In these circumstances, the facilities available to new entrants, certainly in the national field or even in some major provincial centres, are unlikely to be any greater than they are today, and arguably significantly less so.

21 It is with this prospect in mind rather more than for immediate impact that we would envisage the creation of a National Printing Corporation and the creation of a Launch Fund.

22 We feel that such a corporation could assist in the rationalisation of newspaper plant and that the National Printing Corporation starting perhaps on a modest experimental basis could acquire some of the surplus capacity that is now in existence and help to create a useful pool of resources which could be used to encourage the growth of diversity among newspapers. (We might at this stage point out the interesting example of the Cotton Board. In post-war years the Cotton Board was given the task of helping to rationalise the cotton industry and was supplied with government capital and powers to buy up surplus equipment. That equipment was in the main out-of-date and useful only for scrapping.* However, there is no reason why a similar pattern of acquisition could not be used to develop a public corporation for printing. In this case, however, the pool of resources would not be for scrapping but to establish the basis for a competitive public enterprise in the printing industry).

Structure of the National Printing Corporation

23 We would propose that a National Printing Corporation should be a subsidiary of the National Enterprise Board. This would help to ensure:

(a) That there would be no direct state interference in the type of publication accepted for printing by the National Printing Corporation;

(b) That the Corporation would be run on commercial lines as laid down in the terms of reference of the NEB so that although an initial injection of government money would be required for its estabishment, it would seek to become self-financing and commercially viable.

24 We would not wish at this point to make detailed proposals on the precise operation of the National Printing Corporation since we believe that this should be a matter for negotiation

Reorganisation of the Cotton Industry, Cmnd 744—May 1959.

between the NEB and the other interested parties. However, to sketch a rough outline of our thoughts in this respect, we would offer the following ideas:

(a) That 50 per cent of the National Printing Corporation Board should be composed of union members who are employees of the Corporation and that among the other members there should be at least one, perhaps two, members of the Press Council;

(b) That the National Printing Corporation should be empowered to offer assistance to finance initial working capital for new publications on commercial terms and to offer professional, financial and marketing expertise. The NPC would of course also operate, on normal commercial terms, in the general printing market so as to make full use of its printing capacity;

(c) That the sole criteria for refusing a publication should be on the grounds of lack of financial viability, for legal reasons or where a publication could legitimately be considered a threat to national security.

25 So far as the National Printng Corporation is concerned some of the plant they acquired might well be redundant in the same way that the textile plant acquired by the Cotton Board was out-of-date on acquisition. On the other hand there is no reason why the National Printing Corporation should not acquire modern plant which was also surplus to capacity. In this way from a modest pilot-basis the National Printing Corporation could build up an efficient although small public sector in printing, which would introduce a fresh element of competition with the private sector. There would be no question at any time of seeking to establish a monopoly situation in the public sector. This could be written into the initial terms, although the Monopolies Commission powers as they are would appear to be sufficient to prevent this happening.

26 We are well aware that under Section 9 of the Industry Act 1975, the National Enterprise Board is debarred from acquiring

any interest in the field of publishing. However, our proposals concerning the National Printing Corporation do not contravene this Section of the Act. The NPC would be solely concerned with the printing operation, which, as with contract printing in the private sector, would be totally separate from the editorial side. It would not therefore be a publisher within the meaning of Section 9.

Launch Fund

27   We would also propose the establishment of a Launch Fund along similar lines to those advocated in the Hirsch-Gordon scheme* although our proposal is really a variation of Hirsch-Gordon. Our view is that for new publications the launch scheme could operate in the following manner: the initial capital to launch a newspaper whether national or provincial would have to be found through the market or from funds borrowed from the National Printing Corporation on market terms and negotiated in the normal commercial way. Any assistance by way of state loans or subsidies would come into operation only at a second stage. That is to say initial capital would come from private sources and this would carry a new entrant to a point at which its circulation or advertising revenue had reached a given level. At that level it would then qualify for some assistance to enable it to climb over the often fatal barrier of a second stage launch. For example, the Launch Fund could begin to operate in the case of a new daily newspaper when that paper had reached say a circulation of 50,000. A subsidy could then operate for a period until the ciculation had been doubled, but with a specific time limit set. Once the circulation had reached double the figure at which the Launch Fund was triggered the subsidy would begin to diminish and taper off until it was withdrawn completely within an agreed time limit. This would ensure that there was no open-ended subsidy for any publication. We believe the chief importance of such a scheme would be to encourage market support for a broader press diversity. The prospect of this additional assurance towards success could be an important encouragement to the market to provide initial and subsequent funds. One further possibility is that the Launch Fund method

*See reference to Hirsch-Gordon Scheme in the main report (13.12-13.19).

might be linked with the National Printing Corporation and that in such cases the assistance offered through the Launch Fund could be in the form of a printing discount administered by the National Printing Corporation. It has been pointed out to us that there are disadvantages in linking the two schemes together. One of the major disadvantages would be the financial uncertainties about both operations and this might combine to make a joint scheme more difficult to operate than two separate, if not wholly independent, operations.

28   The Majority Report has criticised the general principle of a Launch Fund for each specific type of publication. We therefore think it right that we should reply to these criticisms.

29   The intervention of a Launch Fund for daily newspapers is attacked on grounds of cost, and the losses of *The Times* are cited as an example of how much money would be involved. However, we have made it clear that any subsidy would not be open-ended. Publications would only receive money after they had already been successfully launched with their own money and achieved a certain circulation. The subsidy would end after a set time limit or when a further growth in circulation had been achieved, whichever came earlier. The amount of money involved would therefore be strictly limited for any one publication.

30   It is suggested that in the cases both of provincial daily and weekly newspapers there is now insufficient scope for increased competition. This seems to us a rather negative argument. Our major concern has been to seek ways of increasing diversity and it is for this reason that we support the idea of a Launch Fund. We believe it would be wrong to say that there are no opportunities for diversification in any given area until the resources have been made available for such diversification to be attempted and response adequately tested. We must reiterate that we are not asking for vast sums of public money to be risked. The possibility of a subsidy must act as a spur to the establishment of new publications, but they will not qualify for the subsidy until they have proved with their own resources that there is scope for a successful alternative publication in their particular locality or field.

31 Whichever way financial assistance was offered to the Launch Fund, there would have to be a strict and specific measure applied to the particular type of paper being assisted. For example, the kind of assistance, circulation calculations and the time limit would no doubt have to be different for a new launch national daily paper than for a localised provincial evening paper or a weekly. The Launch Fund would need to be limited to daily, evening or weekly newspapers. Weekly journals of a specialised variety or trade and technical papers would be excluded from any such assistance since their *raison d'etre* is different. And, of course, existing newspapers would not qualify.

32 A comparison has been made between the way a Launch Fund would assist small magazines and the operation of the current Arts Council grants to certain artistic magazines. The conclusion is drawn that the extension of such a system of grants would create a form of censorship. We do not think this is a helpful analogy. The Arts Council's distribution of money—not only to publications, but to all the other functions it supports—is necessarily discriminatory on grounds of artistic value, and may continue on an almost permanent basis (ie the Royal Opera House). The establishment of a Launch Fund for publications would not affect such arrangements. Nor would it increase the danger of censorship, since its operation would depend primarily on objective statistical criteria, and therefore would not involve selectivity on the basis of content or opinions.

33 The Majority Report considers community newspapers, and suggests that the way to help them is by an extension of the practice operated by certain authorities of providing advice and finance. We believe this is inconsistent with the general view taken that *direct* state intervention constitutes a threat to the freedom of the press—a view which we share. If that threat exists at a national level, surely it must exist even more so at a community level, since much of the content of community newspapers is criticism of the relevant local authorities and health authorities, on which many local councillors sit. (The fact that only 11 of the metropolitan authorities gave assistance to community newspapers may well indicate that censorship is already in existence in a negative way.)

34 This paper has sought to combine a general and philosophical critique of the press with some minimum proposals for assisting the process of increased diversity. If we assume that diversity is the central issue in seeking to improve the quality and calibre of the British press then it follows that we should try to encourage this process by practical means,. rather than simply pay lip-service to the concept. Some of those who justifiably criticise the political imbalance of the national and mass circulation newspapers do not in fact wish to see public funds used to improving the newspaper industry as it now exists. They would far rather see the industry degenerate into an even tighter and more firmly closed monopoly and the press, as we know it, destroy itself by what they believe to be a self-perpetuating and ultimately destructive competitive process. What we have tried to do in this brief analysis is to offer some thought on how the press can help to improve itself with the minimum of state assistance.

35   There ought also to be opportunities for the development of producer-press co-operatives embracing journalists, printing staff, administration and clerical workers, possibly with consumer/reader representation on a board. There ought to be greater encouragement for various forms of experiments with a free press. There should be an altogether greater flexibility and freedom for newspapers to emerge so that they can better respond to the developing social and cultural impulses of modern society, without having to depend on the all pervasive influences of mass market pressures which in our view contribute significantly to the inadequacies of our contemporary press. While nobody can forecast what will happen in the future to the various newspaper ownerships, to costs, new technology, advertising revenues or circulation the danger of further contraction (and monopoly) is clearly a very real one. There might be a good deal of scepticism about the viability, in the short term, of what we are suggesting. But in the longer term solutions along the lines we are proposing may well be the only way of guaranteeing the continued existence of a broadly-based democratic press in Britain.

36   Finally, we must emphasise that in putting forward our proposals we do not make any large claims as to what might be achieved by such interventionism.* We have no illusions about the limitations that can, and must, be placed on such experiments. Nor do we believe that even if the experiments proved to be extremely successful they would or could remove all the objectionable features of the press to which critics of all kinds usually allude. But we do believe that a combination of these proposals plus a strengthening of the Press Council will help to achieve a significant improvement.

37   In the end however nothing can achieve this without the collective will of all who work in the press; all who manage, administer and edit our newspapers. We believe that the best among all of them do require and deserve a little help.

> 'The worth of a newspaper lies in the range and accuracy of its information, the common sense of its assessments, the quality of its writing and the wisdom and candour of its views.'
>
> Editorial, *The Times*, 10 June 1959

DAVID BASNETT
GEOFFREY GOODMAN

*See reference in majority report, Chapter 10: Addendum—*Daily Mail*, paragraph 8.

B/031/09/77 Published by the Labour Party, Transport House, Smith Square London SW1P 3JA and printed by Victoria House Printing Co. (T.U.) 25 Cowcross Street, London EC1.